I Can't Untie My Shoes!

by
Bil Keane

FAWCETT CREST • NEW YORK

A School Book Fairs, Inc. Edition

"Well! I don't know what to do today — finger paint or fight with Jeffy."

"It broke. Now all I have is a yo."

"I hit a home run, but I forgot to touch the bases when I was running."

"Nope—you're wrong. I weigh eleventy-teen."

"Jeffy opened all the cans of tennis balls just to hear
them go 'ssss'!"

"When you see the lightning, quick cover your ears so you won't be scared by the thunder."

"I'm not asking Aunt Nancy for a present. I'm just telling her my birthday's coming up."

"Come on in! Mommy's right here —
in the closet."

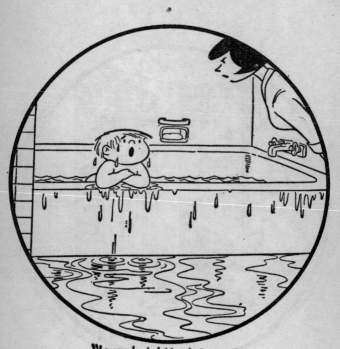

"I was bein' Mark Spitz."

"I saw Dolly HIT a kid. Does that mean
he's her boy friend?"

"People who don't give me anything get turned into a
FROG!"

"We're going right back out again as soon as we
look at the stuff in our bags."

"Mommy pretends she's looking at the size, but she's really looking at the price."

"It's crying 'cause summer is over."

"... And when PJ finally goes to school, you'll
be the only one home to take
care of the frog."

"Oh, no! Mrs. Wilsey will NEVER believe
I did my homework!"

"Their mommies write their names on their shirts so they won't lose them."

"... And this means to go THAT way, horsie!"

"I'm getting very growed up. Already I know
my right foot from my wrong."

"Look, Mommy! They ate up everybody's stuff 'cept
YOURS!"

"I have to sit next to Mommy so I can tell her what's happenin' in the game."

"I can't come out—my grandma and granddad just
got here and I hafta stay in to play
with THEM."

"Not now! Grandma and Granddad have to unpack
and then take a rest."

"This is a HARD way to make pumpkin pie, Grandma. Don't you know how to make the frozen
kind?"

" . . . And you hang your 'jammies right down here."

"I wish the pilgrims had sent out for PIZZA on the first
Thanksgiving 'stead of shootin' a turkey."

"It's okay, Granddad, go back to sleep. I just have to
get something out of the toy box."

"Mommy and Grandma will NEVER get those dishes done 'cause all they do is talk."

"It's okay for you and Granddad to use our beds
'cause Jeffy likes sleeping on the old cot and I
get to sleep on the floor in a SLEEPIN'
BAG!"

"If Grandma is going shopping, too, I'll come with you, but if she's not I think I'll stay home."

"Boy, we're lucky! We've got a LOT of people to kiss good night!"

"Grandma says that's how she used to rock you, but how could she even LIFT you?"

" . . . And over here, Granddad, the swings are broken and the sandbox needs fixin' and the seat is off my bike and . . ."

"Mommy! Will you come here and show Grandma
how to cut our oranges?"

"How did we get to know Grandma and Granddad?"

"But you don't have to see my test paper 'cause
Grandma already signed it."

"Since Grandma and Granddad have been here we haven't sent Daddy out for fried chicken or hamburgers even ONCE!"

"But they HAFTA go home. Grandma wants to clean her OWN house for a change."

"Why are you crying, Grandma? Didn't you enjoy
your visit?"

"Lift me up higher so I can touch his branches."

"...and when I say 'who do you think you're pushing?', you go 'GRRR!' Right, Sam?"

"He's in here sleeping! Shall I wake him up or let him sleep?"

"Fred doesn't chirp any more 'cause he doesn't
want Kittycat to know he's a bird."

"It's Mrs. LaPorta. Shall I ask her if she's returning the eggs she borrowed?"

"It's okay to stay in my room, PJ, 'cause Mommy said you could, but STOP LISTENING TO MY RECORD!"

"Daddy, can you teach me to read? Then I'll be able to tell what's coming on TV."

"We left them there for you to play with."

"It's snowing! Is Santa comin' again?"

"I've got 23 things on my list. How many things
will Santa buy us?"

"Mommy's spelling things on the phone 'cause
Barfy's listening."

"Thel, have you seen my shaving cream?"

"Two, four, six, eight--who do we 'preciate?
Santa Claus! Santa Claus! Hooray!"

"Would you like to order a . . . No, I guess you've got your Christmas reefs already."

"Daddy! Today's the day everybody's puttin' up their
Christmas lights!"

"Did you get my letter, Santa?"

"Yes — Yes, I did."

"That's very good — I mailed it to the North Pole this morning."

"The sun's almost down — can we turn on the outside
lights now?"

"Don't guess that I got socks for you, Daddy."

"'Dear Friends: The high points of our year were Billy's report card and PJ's new tooth. ... How's it sound so far?"

"Mommy, a lady from some store says the doll house you ordered is in."

". . . And how many hours do they estimate THIS
one will last?"

". . . And there was no room for them at the Inn."
"Joseph should've phoned ahead for a reservation."

"P J's not putting them on one at a time."

"Mommy! I know how to make our tree lights
the blinkin' kind!"

"I made it in school, but I only got a 'C' 'cause of the spelling."

"Santa didn't bring me the chemistry set, but that's
okay — I'll ask the Easter Bunny for it."

"Daddy's wearing the socks Jeffy gave him but
he's not wearing the tie I bought him."

"Do I have to thank Aunt Nancy for the archery set?
It's broken already."

"Look at Grandma's funny little tree! The whole thing's WHITE and all the balls are GOLD!"

"Oh, no! Grandma gave us a zoo set 'zactly like the one Santa brought us."

"Mommy, can all those 'tato chips and peanuts and things in the living room be our breakfast?"

"I'm just out here sayin' goodby to our tree."

"That was Mrs. Potter on the phone. I knew you were busy so I told her you were sleeping."

"Can I wake up now?"

"Tell us that story again 'bout how you and Daddy
met and Grandma didn't want you to get married
and 'bout the Christmas you got engaged and how
you made your wedding dress and ..."

"I can't eat any more. I'm saving my crusts for the birds."

"She's talking to Betsy's doll."

"WHY don't you want a Valentine party?"
"'Cause nobody else is havin' one."

"Will you draw a big heart, Mommy? But don't
look at it 'cause it's somethin' I'm makin'
for YOU."

"Everything is very quiet in the winter 'cause the plants are sleeping."

"We saved a little for you to do, Daddy."

"You better cut out that smokin', Sam, or you might die young."

"Hee-hee-hee — it TICKLES, Mommy! Stop ticklin'!"

"When the snow melts, what happens to the white?"

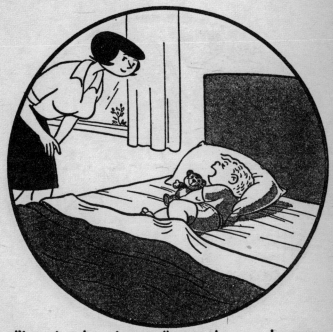

"I was just dreaming — y'know, when you close your
eyes and the picture comes on?"

"Picture books are better than television 'cause you don't miss anything when you go to the bathroom."

"Mrs. Wilsey doesn't want you to help me with my math 'cause you do it the old-fashioned way."

"Billy just said a bad word Do you wanna hear
what it was?"

"But the baby-sitter last night said we could jump on the bed anytime if we take our shoes off first."

"I'm gonna run away from home?"

"Will you zip up my jacket and tie my shoes?"

"Sorry — it's just a can of peaches."

"Could I get a new bike? The one I got for Christmas went out of style."

"Listen — the poor little guy's trying to talk."
"No, he CAN talk! We just can't understand him."

"I know — wash my hands right away and don't touch the walls."

"Why didn't they have her booked for illegal entry?"

"Do you want to buy ten boxes of candy, Mommy?
That's all I have left out of twelve."

"Grandma is buying five boxes of my candy — one
for her and one for each of US."

"Mommy! Daddy's touching the little screwdriver that
goes with your sewing machine!"

"Wait! Dummy! Put the candy in your mouth
FIRST! THEN ask if you can have a piece!"

"Daddy, when Lincoln was runnin' for president, did you vote for him or the other guy?"

"It's called RELAXIN'. It's something cats know how to
do better than anybody else."

"Watch how good I can karate this pasghetti."

"You better not treat her mean, Jeffy, 'cause you're her UNCLE!"

"Give me a word with a lot of Ss and Xs in it. We're learning those letters in school right now."

"People are always callin' me Jeffy, and they call
Jeffy, Billy. Don't we look like OURSELVES?"

"We watered the living room plants for you."

"Couldn't you go later, Daddy? We're having a club meeting."

"Mommy, will you change channels for me? I don't
want to disturb Kittycat."

"When Granddad went to heaven did he ever write
back and tell us how he likes it?"

"Some of Steve's grape soda sprayed on the new drapes but it's okay 'cause he said he was sorry."

"Mommy! Will you tell Jeffy these flowers are artificial? He won't believe me."

"Stand up, Daddy! They're playin' our nashnul an-fum."

"Know what? I think Miss Elaine has eyes in the top of her head, too."

"I do SO know how to tell time! It's three pounds after two."

"I'll do my other homework later. This is my GYM homework."

"I made up a connect-the-dots picture, but when I connected the dots, nothing came out."

"God doesn't answer — maybe he left the phone off the hook."

"When you said I could bring somebody home with me, how many somebodies did you mean?"

"The second fork is there in case you drop the first one."

"Boy! This new chair of yours is REALLY comfortable,
right, Daddy?"

"Mummies are dead people all wrapped up in bandages and they live in guitar cases."

"I don't have to use a booster seat at Grandma's. She
lets me sit on the phone book."

"What channel shall I put your 'lectric blanket on?"

"Mommy, did you ever fall in love with anybody?"

EDITOR'S NOTE: Billy, Dolly, Jeffy, and PJ wanted to help Daddy with this book, so they drew the cartoon for this page.